BERLIN

POTSDAM

Sanssouci

DEM DEUTSCHEN VOLKE

RV Rahmel-Verlag

www.rahmel-verlag.de

INTRODUCTION

Welcome to one of the most beautiful, fascinating, contradictory, exciting, lively and culturally open cities in Europe and the world. Berlin is one of those great metropolises that resist precise definition. It is too large and too complex to be contained in few words. While it does have 750 years of history behind it, if you are expecting a noble, elderly matron placidly sitting on her laurels, you couldn't be more wrong. In Berlin, majestic 18th century monuments nestle modern works of mind-blowing architecture, precious historic art collections and the famed Berliner Philharmoniker stand alongside galleries that attract all of the artistic avant-garde techno music fans, the quiet Schlosspark alongside the mad chaos of Kurfürstendamm, the pompous Soviet monuments alongside the gigantic Molecule Man whose shadows stretches over Treptow, the tradition of old cafes alongside the bright lights of the hottest nightspots. But this is no hodge-podge. It is Berlin with its magical ability to harmonize, transform and evolve.

The city arose in the 13th century on the shores of the Spree in an area of the Brandenburg conceded to the Ascanian dynasty by emperor Lotharius. In the same period, another center, Cölln, arose in the same area with which Berlin

◀ **Brandenburg Gate**

▲ Reichstag

Dome of the Reichstag ▶

quickly formed an alliance. In the following century, the two towns bore the brunt of conflicts for the possession of Brandenburg that started after the death of the last Margrave of the Ascanian family line. Two terrible fires also ravaged the towns.

In 1411, the ascent of Frederick VI Hohenzollern as the leader of Brandenburg, of which he was named Grand Elector by Sigismund, seemed to assure the area a period of peace. Berlin and Cölln grew and prospered under these favorable conditions and in 1432 they united into a single city. In 1447 Berlin rebelled against Frederick II, the successor to Frederick I. He crushed the revolt and chose the city as his residence.

Some fifty years, Joachim II, who had converted to Lutheranism in 1539, had a confluence built between the Spree and the Havel, the fortified citadel of Spandau to whose construction German and foreign artists contributed. This flurry of activity was abruptly interrupted by the outbreak of a terrible epidemic of the Plague that decimated the population of Berlin and left it in grave social and economic conditions. The Thirty Year War further exacerbated the situation, making its tragic effects felt in the early part of the 17th century.

A few years before the war's end, the city took important steps on the road to recovery, thanks mainly to Frederick Wilhelm, the Great Prince Elector under whom Berlin managed to become a major cultural and commercial center, welcoming the two important communities with the Jewish people and Huguenots who escaped from France in 1685.

The period of great flourishing continued under the reign of his son Frederick III, later self-proclaimed as the King of Prussia with the name of Frederick I. During this period, Berlin experienced a strong surge in construction as well as artistic, cultural and scientific activity.

After an almost militaristic rigidity imposed during the period of the son of Frederick

I, Frederick Wilhelm I, Berlin experienced astonishing development in almost all fields starting in 1740 with the ascent to the throne of Frederick II, the Great. These highly favorable conditions let Frederick the Great undertake major works of organizing and beautifying the city. During his reign, Berlin also increased its importance in the cultural and intellectual realms and became one of the main centers of the European Enlightenment.

This exceptional period did not end with Frederick II. It continued for the entire first half of the 19th century, despite the interlude of the Napoleonic occupation. Alongside cultural development with the growth of Romanticism and the foundation of the Humboldt Universität, there was architectural devel-

DEUTSCHEN VOLKE

opment dominated by the figure of Karl Friedrich Schinkel and industrial development that developed in step with the city's modernization.

However, as in the rest of Europe, in Berlin, rapid industrial development triggered a series of social problems that found expression in large demonstrations and demands by workers. In March 1848, to break up a protest demonstration, the military opened fire on the people, killing 250.

Already ruling since 1858 for his brother Frederick Wilhelm IV, who was of infirm mind, Wilhelm I took the throne in 1861. A year later, to contend with pressures from liberals and progressives, he named Otto von Bismarck prime minister. With his "Realpolitik", which cost two wars (against Austria and France), the future chancellor of the Reich managed to impose the absolute supremacy of Prussia with the appointment of Wilhelm I as emperor of Germany on January 18, 1871 in Versailles.

As the city had risen to the ranks of a capital of the kingdom and imperial residence, from that point until 1890, having become a full-fledged modern metropolis, Berlin experienced first hand the advent of the German Reich and the ups and downs of Bismarkian politics, which found itself contending with increasingly fierce Socialist opposition.

Wilhelm II's ascent to the throne and the resulting dismissal of Bismarck did not greatly change the social situation in Berlin. Worsened by the effects of World

▲ **Humboldt University**

War I, it created the perfect conditions for the expression of popular discontent in the form of strikes and protests in the squares.

On November 9, 1918 the increasingly strong conflict between social democrats and communists reached its peak. The Social Democrat Philipp Scheidemann and the leader of the Communist party Karl Liebknecht simultaneously proclaimed one a republic and the other a socialist republic. Wilhelm II was forced to choose exile in Holland. The situation exploded in January 1919 in Berlin with the Spartacist revolution, bloodily squashed by government troops and the militias of nationalist volunteers which took advantage of the unrest to assassinate Rosa Luxemburg and Karl Liebknecht.

In August of the same year, the proclamation of the constitution and the republic of Weimar seemed to assure a period of relative social rest. Yet, the continuous strife between the oppositions and an economic

◄ **Unter den Linden - Equestrian monument of Frederick the Great**

▲ **Pariser Platz**

crisis of colossal proportions made themselves felt in Berlin too. Despite everything, for Berlin, the 1920s were years of the dolce vita in its cultural flourishing, the triumph of cinema and the development of a great, new

theatre tradition. Nonetheless, the dark shadow of National Socialism began to stretch over the city.

On January 30, 1933, the SA celebrated the appointment of Hitler as chancellor of the Reich with the

▼ **Unter den Linden - Zeughaus**

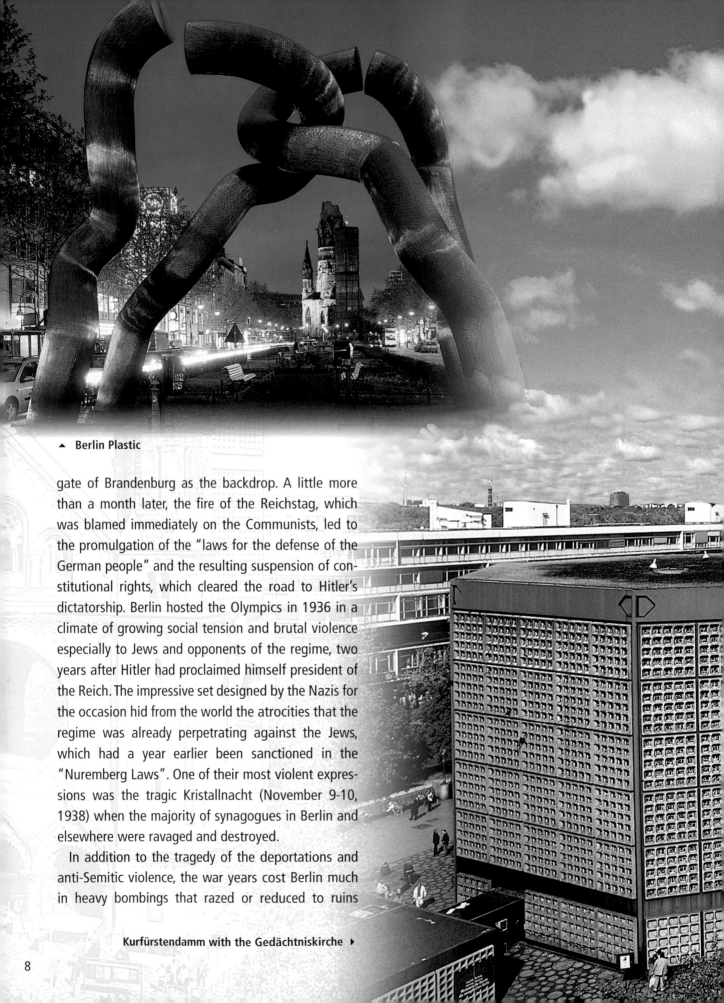

▲ **Berlin Plastic**

gate of Brandenburg as the backdrop. A little more than a month later, the fire of the Reichstag, which was blamed immediately on the Communists, led to the promulgation of the "laws for the defense of the German people" and the resulting suspension of constitutional rights, which cleared the road to Hitler's dictatorship. Berlin hosted the Olympics in 1936 in a climate of growing social tension and brutal violence especially to Jews and opponents of the regime, two years after Hitler had proclaimed himself president of the Reich. The impressive set designed by the Nazis for the occasion hid from the world the atrocities that the regime was already perpetrating against the Jews, which had a year earlier been sanctioned in the "Nuremberg Laws". One of their most violent expressions was the tragic Kristallnacht (November 9-10, 1938) when the majority of synagogues in Berlin and elsewhere were ravaged and destroyed.

In addition to the tragedy of the deportations and anti-Semitic violence, the war years cost Berlin much in heavy bombings that razed or reduced to ruins

Kurfürstendamm with the Gedächtniskirche ▶

◄ **Potsdamer Platz - Sony-Center**   ▲ **Potsdamer Platz - Panorama**

almost the entire city, taking a great many victims. Hitler's suicide in his bunker in Potsdamer Platz officially marked the collapse of the regime. Two years later, on May 2, 1945, the city, reduced to a desolate heap of rubble, was occupied by Soviet troops.

After the unconditional surrender, signed May 8, 1945, the city was divided into four sections assigned to the victorious powers, whose alliance after the end of the war lasted only very briefly. The serious differences that divided France, England and the United States on one side from the Soviet Union on the other, between 1948 and 1949, led to the blockage of Berlin and then the proclamation of the German Federal Republic (May 23) and the German Democratic Republic with the East Berlin capital (October 7). Now starkly divided, in the next fifty years the two Berlins followed very different paths, marked by a major economic split and a social situation in the eastern section that lived through the politics of repression implemented by the authorities.

In 1961, to try to impede the escape of its inhabitants to the West, the authorities of East Berlin decided to build the Wall, which cut the city in two until 1989. Partly mitigated by ongoing international diplomacy, this closure and segregation policy ended definitively on November 9, 1989, with the historic decision by the RDT to reopen the boundary between the two sections of the city. The images of the fall of the Wall traveled the world, attesting to the end of one of the darkest eras in Berlin's history.

After the reunification of the two Germanies, sealed on August 31, 1990, on June 20 of the following year, Berlin was declared the capital, returning it to the central role which it had earned over its many centuries of history.

BRANDENBURGER TOR

The **Brandenburger Tor (Brandenburg Gate)**, a monument that symbolizes Berlin, was built in 1789, under Frederick Wilhelm II, by Carl Gotthard Langhans. The majestic monument's prestigious position at the end of the Unter den Linden made it long the definitive reference point for the city and later the symbol of its reunification. The architect took inspiration from the entrance of the Acropolis of Athens for its design.

The result is an elegant neoclassical building of impressive dimensions; 26 meters high, including the chariot on the top, 65.5 meters wide and 11 meters deep. The frontal colonnade, consisting of six mighty Doric columns, marks the five opening of the gate, separated by thick walls. The four side openings, each of which is nearly four meters wide, frame the 5.65 wide large central passage, which was originally reserved for the passage of the royal court. The two side wings to the right and left of the gate held the garrisons of guard soldiers and the lodgings of royal tax collectors. Some seventy years after its opening in the summer of 1791, the gate was remodeled

by Johann Heinrich Strack with the addition of two colonnade passages connecting the gate and the side wings.

Between the 18th and 19th centuries, Johann Gottfried Schadow designed most of the monument's decorations. He was also the artist of the elegant quadriga that crowns

the gate. The chariot, pulled by four horses, is guided by the winged goddess of Victory.

The Brandenburger Tor is the only surviving of Berlin's eighteen original gates. In its long history as witness and symbol of the power of Germany, with the construction of the Wall that ran immediately west of it in 1961, it became the very image of the division between East and West Berlin. It was then reopened at the end of 1989. A year later it was the center of grand celebrations at the fall of the Wall and reunification.

REICHSTAGSGEBÄUDE AND SURROUNDINGS

The building was commissioned to the architect Paul Wallot after the proclamation of the German empire on January 18, 1871, for the purpose of providing accommodations befitting the new parliament. Between 1884 and 1894 Wallot, made a majestic complex in neoclassical style consisting of two buildings connected by a tunnel and crowned in the center by a grand cupola. In February 1933, a fire, whose cause and blame are still not completely clear, ravished a large part of the building, which was abandoned by the parliament. Reichstagsgebäude had lost its role of a central hub of Germany's political life and was not even restored after the fire. At the end of World War II, it was heavily bombed and then pillaged. The dome, which was still reigning over the spectral ruins of the building, was blown up in 1954. The restoration work was started in 1961 and only finished a decade later, without the dome, and it was returned to its original function. On December 20, 1990, it held the first session of the parliament of the reunified Germany. In 1995, the building was spectacularly wrapped by the artist Christo and Jeanne Claude with thousands of meters of fabric. The following restoration, directed by the English architect Norman Foster, radically changed the interior appearance of the Reichstagsgebäude, while leaving the outside structure unaltered. The new building is ultra-modern with its most spectacular element the majestic dome that sits atop the hall of the plenary assembly. The structure is made entirely of glass, 23 meters high with a 40 meter diameter. Inside it has an upside down cone covered in 360 mirrors. The dome can be seen from much of the city and can be admired close up by climbing to the scenic terrace

▲ Reichstag plenary assembly hall

Reichstag with dome ▶

on the building's roof. It offers both a breathtaking view over Berlin and a pleasant outdoor restaurant that is open for lunch and dinner.

DEM DEUTSCHEN VOLKE

The **Bundeskanzleramt (Federal Chancellery)**, to the north, is one of the most interesting of the nearby parliamentary buildings.

▲ Federal Chancellery

The **Lehrter Stadtbahnhof** is also to the north of the Reichstagsgebäude, designed by the architect Meinhard von Gerkan of Hamburg to hold Berlin's new central railway station, a grand futuristic structure that welcomes over 60 million travelers a year.

◀ Reichstag, ray of light on the crystal dome

▼ Lehrter Stadtbahnhof

PARISER PLATZ

The square in front of Brandenburger Tor has undergone major restoration, rebuilding and construction that has restored it to its pre-World War II status and splendor. Interesting renovations include those of the famous **Hotel Adlon**, on the corner with Wilhelmstraße, and those directed by the architect J.P. Kleihues of the Haus Sommer and the Haus Liebermann, to the two sides of the Brandenburg Gate, which has become the headquarters of major banking groups including **DZ Bank**.

▼ **Hotel Adlon**   **DZ Bank** ▶

UNTER DEN LINDEN

At the opposite end from the Brandenburger Tor, the Pariser Platz accesses Berlin's most famous avenue, the **Unter den Linden**. Lined by grand buildings, the large thoroughfare is 60 m wide and almost a kilometer and a half long, and extends to the Schlossbrücke, from which Schlossplatz is entered. Originally, a country path ran this course. In the 16th century, the Prince Elector used it to reach the Tiergarten, the hunting reserve then located at the edges of the city. Around the mid 17th century, on the orders of Grand Elector Frederick Wilhelm, the

‹ Unter den Linden - Equestrian monument of Frederick the Great

route was embellished with rows of walnut and linden trees. The walnuts died and were placed by other lindens. During World War II, all the trees were cut down, and new lindens were not planted until 1946.

The construction development of the large avenue only properly began at the beginning of the following century, when Frederick the Great ordered the construction of many prestigious buildings that gave the Unter den Linden its splendor and elegance, befitting a thoroughfare that connected the city's castle with the Tiergarten. The work was crowned at the end of the century with the erection of the Brandenburger Tor.

▲ Detail of equestrian monument of Frederick the Great

Proceeding from Pariser Platz in the direction of Schlossplatz, you pass the **Russische Botschaft** on the right, an elegant building from the early part of the 18th century. Around 1840, it was acquired by Czar Nicholas I, who had it restored and embellished. With the end of the Czarist empire, the building became the headquarters of the Soviet embassy. It was completely destroyed by bombings during World War II. Rebuilt in the early 1950s, it continued to hold the Soviet embassy to the RDT until the fall of the wall and reunification. The Russian embassy is currently located here.

Passing the area of embassies, which includes the British, Polish and Hungarian embassies, we reach the intersection with Friedrichstraße, once the site of famous fashionable night spots which have since dis-

▼ **French embassy**

appeared along with the buildings that held them, which have been restructured and adapted for different uses. For instance, in place of the famed Café Bauer is the French Cultural Center, while the equally famous Café Cranzler, on the opposite side, was replaced by a modern building adjacent to the prestigious Grand Hotel.

On the left of the following intersection with Charlottenstraße, the Unter den Linden has one of its most impressive monuments in the **Staatsbibliothek**. In neo-Baroque style, it was built between 1903 and 1914 by Ernst von Ihne on the site of the former Marstall, the headquarters of the Academy of Sciences and the Academy of Fine Arts built at the end of the 17th century by J. A. Nering and Martin Grünberg. The new building was used to house the Königliche Bibliothek, which was rechristened the Preußische

▼ State library (Staatsbibliothek)

▲ Equestrian monument of Frederick the Great

Staatsbibliothek after World War I. During the years of Nazism and World War II, part of the library's collection, consisting of about four million volumes, was spread in various points in Berlin and other cities. With the division of Berlin, the volumes were not gathered in a single point, but concentrated in two different sites, the one on the Unter den Linden, which took the name Deutsche Staatsbibliothek, and one in West Berlin, named the Staatsbibliothek Preußischer Kulturbesitz and housed in the Kulturforum since the 1980s. With reunification, while continuing to keep

◀ Detail of equestrian monument of Frederick the Great

Humboldt University (Humboldt Universität) ▶

two separate sites, the two large libraries were administratively unified in the Staatsbibliothek zu Berlin - Preußischer Kulturbesitz.

In addition to the library, the **grand equestrian statue of Frederick the Great (Reiterdenkmal Friedrichs des Großen)**, made between 1839 and 1851 by Christian Daniel Rauch, stands tall in the center of the Unter den Linden. On its high pedestal, divided into three levels, there are the names of illustrious contemporaries of the king and life-size statues of his generals, artists, scientists and political men of the era along with ornate bas-relief panels with episodes from the king's life.

Further up also on the left, stands **Humboldt Universität**, adorned by the statues of Alexander and Wilhelm von Humboldt in front of the entry door. Designed by G. Wenzeslaus von Knobelsdorff in the mid 18th century for Prince Henry, the brother of Frederick the Great, it was donated to the university by Frederick Wilhelm in 1810. In addition to its founder, Wilhelm von Humboldt, the institution can boast many prestigious names of German culture in its historic roster of professors, including the philosophers Fichte, Feuerbach, Hegel and Schleiermacher, the brothers Grimm and the scientists Albert Einstein and Max Planck.

Right in front of the university, Micha Ullmann's original modern monument (1995) marks with its underground library room, deserted and stripped of books the place where the Nazis burned mountains of books considered subversive on May 10, 1933. The work was built in the center of Bebelplatz, the heart of the Forum Fridericianum ordered by Frederick the Great, of which the only remainder would have been the Staatsoper court.

▲ **Old Library (Alte Bibliothek)**

The **Alte Bibliothek**, built between 1775 and 1780, is along the western side of the square. The building's original curved façade was designed by Fischer von Erlach and was destroyed in the fire of 1945 and rebuilt in the late 1960s. The nearby Alte Palais on Unter den Linden held the residence of Wilhelm I until 1888 and now belongs to Humboldt Universität.

The eastern side of Bebelplatz is occupied by the **Staatsoper**, conceived in neoclassical forms by G.W. von Knobelsdorff between 1741 and 1743 and reconstructed by Langhans a century later following damage caused by a fire. The building was hit again by a fire in 1941, restored and damaged again during the war. It was renovated in the early 1950s and opened in September of 1955. Now, the Staatsoper has been further renovated following modern architectural criteria, and is able to accommodate about 1,500 spectators for a full bill of operas, ballets, musicals and concerts.

The elegant **Operncafé** to the east is part of the Kronprinzessinenpalais, the 18th century Baroque building that holds the residence of the crown princesses, daughters of Wilhelm III. In the early 19th century, the building was connected with a passage to

◀ **State Opera Hall (Staatsoper)**

▲ Palace of the Crown Prince

▼ Palace of the Princesses (Opernpalais)

the nearby Kronprinzenpalais, made in the latter part of the 17th century by remodeling a pre-existing building. In 1733, Frederick Wilhelm I had it rebuilt in Baroque style for the crown prince. Further modified and expanded, in 1856 the building was occupied by Frederick III and his wife. In 1859 it saw the birth of Wilhelm I. Severe damage inflicted during World War II required complete reconstruction, which was directed by Richard Paulick in the late 1960s. On August 31, 1990 the reunification treaty of the two Germanies was officially signed in its halls.

Behind the Staatsoper, the **Sankt-Hedwigs Kathedrale**, seat of the Catholic bishop of Berlin, is reminiscent of the dome on the Pantheon in Rome. Frederick II commissioned its construction to Johann Boumann in 1747, based on a design by G.W. von Knobelsdorff. It was built right in the middle of the

▲ Neue Wache

▲ Neue Wache (detail of front)

Forum Fridericianum as a demonstration of his toler-
ant spirit to the Catholics.

▼ St.-Hedwigs Kathedrale

On the opposite side next to Humboldt Universität,
the **Neue Wache**, a small, stern building preceded by
a colonnade facade decorated by a gable, was
designed in 1816-18 by Karl Friedrich Schinkel to hold
a guard post. Turned into a monument to the fallen of
World War I in 1931, in 1960 it was assigned by the
RDT authorities to hold the remains of a deportee who
died in a concentration camp and an unknown soldier
and it became a monument to the victims of fascism
and militarism. After the reunification it was declared
a memorial of unified Germany.

The **Zeughaus** is right next to it and the largest of
the Baroque buildings of the Frederick I era that has
survived to this day. Over the long years of its construction (1695-1730) the architects who succeeded

one another in directing the works were the caliber of Nering, Grünberg, Schlüter and Jean de Bodt, the creator of the long, spectacular cantilever facade. The building has a square floor plan spread over two levels and is embellished by interesting decorations including twenty-two beautiful dying warrior masks made by Schlüter that adorn the internal courtyard. The **Zeughaus** served as an arsenal until 1877 when it used first as a museum of arms and then, since 1952, the Museum Deutscher Geschichte, the RDT's history museum incorporated after reunification in the Deutsches Historisches Museum (German History Museum).

On the Schinkelplatz in front of it, after the Minister of Foreign Affairs of the Democratic Republic building was demolished in 1995, on its site the splendor of the historic Bauakademie, the academy of architecture, was built by Schinkel between 1832 and 1836 and then demolished in 1962 after being severely damaged during the war. Across from the square, adorned by a monument to the great architect, the statue of the Baron von Stein is the highest expression of the art of Hermann Schievelbein, the Berlin sculptor representative of the Rauch school who made it in 1860-64.

Beyond the Schinkelplatz, the **Schlossbrücke** crosses a branch of the Spree called Kupfergraben, marking the eastern boundary of the Unter den Linden, which connects to the Schlossplatz. The bridge built by Schinkel between 1822 and 1824 on the site of a previous wooden bridge is lined by elegant perforated cast iron interspersed at the top of the columns by tall white marble pedestals that bear figures of the goddesses Athena, Iris, Minerva and Nike.

◄ Zeughaus – German History Museum

Schlössbrücke with 8 statues of warriors and Greek gods.

▲ Jungfernbrücke (last drawbridge in Berlin) and the Ministry of Foreign Affairs behind it

Altes Museum

MUSEUMSINSEL

Beyond the Schlossbrücke, the vast clearing of the Lustgarten on the left was created in the 16th century to house the vegetable gardens that supplied the kitchens of the Stadtschloss, the building built between 1443 and 1451 on the orders of Frederick II. In 1643, it was decided to turn the area into a park, though it did not lose its original function as a vegetable garden, as on this land a few years later, the first potato plants of Prussia were planted. Because of its position in the city center, Frederick Wilhelm I later decided to use the Lustgarten to put on military parades. In the mid 19th century, the area was again set up as a park.

Today the Lustgarten serves as a scenic frame to the Museumsinsel, the island of museums. Bordered on one side by the Spree and by the Kupfergraben on the other, the complex holds Berlin's oldest and most prestigious museums. It was created on the orders of Frederick Wilhelm III around the **Altes Museum**, built between 1824-1830 by Frederick Wilhelm III to house the royal art collections in an institution open to the public. Between 1843 and the beginning of the 20th century, first the Neues Museum, then the Alte Nationalgalerie and the Bodemuseum were built behind the Altes Museum. The Pergamonmuseum stands between the Bodemuseum and Neues Museum. Its construction was started in 1910 and only completed in 1930. During the bombings of World War II, all of the Museumsinsel buildings bore severe damage – some of them, such as the Neues Museum, were almost completely destroyed – while their collections were fortunately saved having been moved as a precaution and divided among other buildings in the city. At the end of the war, the division of the city made it impossible to recover the entire collection of the island of museums and return

Altes Museum - Detail of an equestrian statue (Löwenbezwinger) ▶

the individual works to the buildings that originally housed them. They remained spread among different institutions in East and West Berlin for years. After the reunification, the new political and administrative situation created the conditions needed to address the issue of recovering and replacing the various museum holdings. With this situation, the Berlin authorities decided to organize the collections of antiquity and archeology in the Museumsinsel buildings and trans-fer the paintings and works of the Gemäldegalerie to the Kulturforum. During this reorganization, it was also decided to undertake major restoration works, modernizing and expanding the museum spaces; some of these works are still underway.

The Altes Museum, built between 1823 and 1830 on the design of Karl Friedrich Schinkel, faces the Lustgarten with its majestic portico with eighteen Ionic columns, entered by a grand stairway preceded

▼ Alte Nationalgalerie

by a large granite pool made by C. Gottlieb Cantian, the Granitschale. The structure, conceived by Schinkel, has a rectangular floor plan and was inspired by the large classic temples of ancient Greece.

It contains a central rotunda on the model of the Pantheon in Rome and is surrounded by a gallery marked by Corinthian columns. The museum, restored in the 1960s, is organized around the original core of Frederick Wilhelm III's Antiquarium to which numerous ancient findings of inestimable value have been added over the years. The museum spaces, part of which are temporarily occupied by a selection of the major works of the **Alte Nationalgalerie** transferred here during restoration and repair work on the building, provide a vast overview of ancient art, starting for the Archaic era ranging over the classic and imperial periods of the Greek and Roman cultures with findings from many centers, including Athens, Corinth, Sparta, Cyclades, Samos, Miletus, Priene and Pergamum. Other points of considerable interest include the collections of materials brought to light during the numerous excavation campaigns undertaken in the 19th and 20th century by Berlin museums.

Directly behind the grand Schinkel museum, the Neues Museum was designed by Friedrich August Stüler and built between 1841 and 1846 to house collections of Egyptian art. Of the buildings in the Museumsinsel, this one suffered the worst damage during World War II. Reconstruction and restoration works were only started in 1985 and are scheduled for completion in 2009. Then, the new museum spaces will be set aside to hold both the Egyptian art collections transferred to the Ägyptisches Museum and

▲ Alte Nationalgalerie – Equestrian monument

▼ **Pergamonmuseum**

PERGAMONMUSEUM

those currently held at the nearby Bodemuseum.

Stüler, in collaboration with Johann Heinrich Strack, is also responsible for the Alte Nationalgalerie, designed as a majestic Corinthian temple elevated on a high basement and erected between 1866 and 1876. The scenic double stairway that accesses the building leads to a grand entrance doorway, dominated by an equestrian monument of Frederick Wilhelm IV added in 1886. The war years deeply impacted the building, which was seriously damaged, as well as its rich collection of gallery paintings, the majority of which went up in smoke during the fire that destroyed the Friedrichshain rooms where they were moved to save them from the bombings. The Alte Nationalgalerie has recently undergone radical restoration and renovation work and now holds

great masterpieces of 19th century painting and sculpture. The displayed works range from Peter Cornelius to Waldmüller, from Schadow to von Hildebrand, from Constable to Courbet and von Menzel, from Leistikow to Max Beckmann, and include the famous Isle of the Dead by Arnold Böcklin, Adolf Hitler's favorite painting.

The **Pergamonmuseum**, built between 1910 and 1930 on the design of Alfred Messel and Ludwig Hoffmann, is probably the most visited of the museums in the complex. It owes its name to the majestic Pergamo altar that it contains, a stately marble work from the 180-159 BC brought to light in the famous city of the Asia Minor (the modern Bergama in Turkey) in the 1880s and then rebuilt stone by stone in Berlin starting in 1902. Preceded by a grand staircase is an

▼ **Pergamonmuseum**

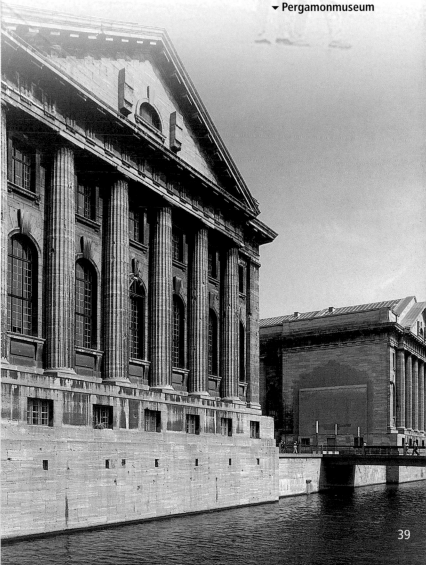

▲ Pergamonmuseum - Altar of Pergamum

altar dedicated to Zeus and Athena, surrounded by a spectacular 120 meter long marble frieze portraying the battle between the gods and the giants, kept on the ground floor of the Antikensammlung building. Works of inestimable value are found in this section, including the gate of the market of Miletus (circa 130 BC) and the splendid floor mosaic of Orpheus (late second century BC), next to which precious Greek and Roman era sculptures and an interesting collection of Hellenistic works are displayed. Also on the ground floor are the vast spaces of the Vorderasiatisches Museum, entirely dedicated to Middle Eastern art and culture, providing a

◄ Pergamonmuseum - Ischtar Tor

comprehensive overview of works and findings that cover a period of some six millennia. The rich collection of art works, furnishings and objects of everyday use belonging mainly to the Nabucodonosor II age are framed by the majestic Ischtar gate (580 BC), a processional road and important fragments of the façade of the throne hall of Babylonia. Finally, the upper floor of the Pergamonmuseum is occupied by the Museum für Islamische Kunst, created in 1904 to hold the façade of the castle of the Mshatta desert, in modern day Jordan, gifted to Wilhelm II by the Turkish sultan at the beginning of the century. Over the years, the museum has collected prestigious items of Islamic art including the Aleppo Room (16th-17th century) and other architectural works, as well as fine pieces of art and craftwork (including fine carpets) from India and Persia.

The **Bodemuseum** was named after Wilhelm von Bode, the former director of Berlin's museums, who founded this museum as well as the Pergamonmuseum when he held this prestigious role. It is set in a splendid building built between 1897 and 1904 at the southern end of the island of museums to which Ernst von Ihne gave its elegant neo-Baroque style. At the end of the restoration works being done on the museum, it will give visitors the chance to admire an impressive collection of Egyptian art, including architectural fragments, funeral outfits, statues, paintings and jewels, as well as fine art works from the Byzantine area, a rich collection of sculptures and the largest collection of antique coins in Europe.

◀ Bodemuseum

BERLINER DOM

The **cathedral of Berlin**, built between 1894 and 1905 by Julius Carl Raschdorff, was ordered by the emperor Wilhelm II to hold the main temple of Prussian Protestantism and the tombs of members of the Hohenzollern dynasty. The grandiose building stands on the site of the existing cathedral designed by Schinkel, the only remaining part of which is the altarpiece by Carl Begas. The original layout of Raschdorff's construction actually included three churches: a northern one that was later destroyed, a southern one dedicated to the celebration of baptisms and weddings of members of the court and a central one, the monumental Predigtkirche, for listening to sermons, able to hold up to 2,000 worshippers. Because of severe damage sustained during World War II, the building had to be partially rebuilt and restored. To give an idea of the Predigtkirche's colossal proportions (116 meter high, 115 meters long, 73 meters wide and topped by a dome coming to almost 75 meters high), consider that it houses an organ with over 7000 pipes! The majestic, highly decorated imperial stairway gives access to the church, and makes it possible to climb the dome, which provides a spectacular panoramic view of the city's roofs.

▲ **Berlin Cathedral - Altar**

POTSDAMER PLATZ

The largest open-air architecture workshop in the world. That is what Potsdamer Platz has been called. The square in the center of the city was the symbol of the Berlin dolce vita in the 1920s and 30s. Bustling with life, full of traffic and people, **Potsdamer Platz** welcomed famed personages such as Greta Garbo and the members of the European elite in its stylish cafes, famous restaurants and exclusive restaurants, which helped create the myth of Berlin in those years. Possibly more than any other place in Berlin, this square best embodies the turbulent and fascinating history of this city during the 20th century, a city able to rise again with incredible energy and enthusiasm from the ashes in which the Hitler era, the war, and the years of the Communist regime and those of the crises following the reunification of the two Germanies had flung it. The lights and shining splendor that animated

it in the 1920s and 30s were first darkened by the sinister shadow of Nazism, represented here in all of its ferocity by the site of the Volksgerichtshof, the people's court ordered by Hitler, then violently cut off by the war bombings which destroyed it, erasing almost all signs of its past glory. Underneath the square, where the Führerbunker was built, the Nazi dictatorship collapsed to the sound of Adolf Hitler's gunshots as he killed himself, putting an end to his barbarous life and the tragedy of the war. Gutted and annihilated by the bombs, its position as a central hub between the eastern and western sections of the city led Potsdamer Platz to be subjected to a further injury with the construction of the Wall, that ran over two levels to prevent any attempts of escape to the West through underground tunnels dug by the Nazis under the square. The entrances of the S-Bahn were also

▲ Potsdamer Platz: Daimler-City Marlene-Dietrich Platz

walled up to prevent any escape. The Potsdamer Platz station became one of the "ghost stations" of the Berlin underground. The square was abandoned for years and constantly guarded by armed cars and armed surveillance posts. After the reunification, it was immediately included in the city areas to be repaired and restored. Nonetheless, the authorities quickly saw that its reconstruction – a total reconstruction, as practically nothing had survived – would require not only considerable expense, but a wide-ranging project entrusted to great architects. To solve the first dilemma, it decided, not without encountering fierce criticism, to sell several lots of land to a group of large investors who could provide

▼ Potsdamer Platz - Panorama

the funds needed for its reconstruction. The second problem was handled by putting up an international competition which was won by two architects from Munich, Hilmer and Sattler. Daimler-Chrysler, Sony, Hertie, ABB and Haus Vaterland AG, the main investors involved in the project, found the solutions proposed by the Germans as too traditional. As no conditions whatsoever had been set by the authorities, they decided to call in another architect to whom to entrust the revision of the urban plan and to commission professionals of their choice to make the constructions planned for the square. Alongside the famous English architect Richard Rogers, the "deus ex machina" of the new Potsdamer Platz, other world-famous architects including Renzo Piano, Arata Isozaki, Rafael Moneo, Helmut Jahn and Giorgio Grassi who reinvented the image of the square, giving rise to buildings and entire complexes that they infused with their originality and artistic genius. In October 1998, **Daimler City** was inaugurated, a neighborhood of over 100,000 square meters intended mainly for commercial activities and some luxury residential use. In addition to the prestigious Grand-Hyatt-Berlin Hotel by Rafael Moneo, the spectacular Potsdamer Platz **Arkaden**, financed by Daimler-Chrysler includes an IMAX hall located in an original spherical construction and the Musical Theater, designed by Renzo Piano

▲ **Potsdamer Platz: Daimler-City Potsdamer-Platz Arkaden**

inspired by the forms of the adjacent Staatsbibliothek. The area entrusted to Helmut Jahn by Sony is also of exceptional originality. Its vast, scenic square covered by a large canvas incorporated part of the historic Hotel Esplanade which survived the war bombings, including the famous Kaisersaal where Wilhelm II liked to entertain. One of the interior facades

of the area holds a giant screen that broadcasts updated news of the world 24 hours a day. The Filmhaus, a structure dedicated to cinema and its history, is also part of the complex.

◀ **Potsdamer Platz Sony Area, DB-Tower**

PHILHARMONIE

The **Philharmonie** stands to Potsdamer Platz's immediate west in the area of Kulturforum. It was built between 1960-1963 on Scharoun's design to create a location worthy of the famous Berliner Philharmoniker. The building is topped by a tent roof and is designed on asymmetrical lines. Inside it holds a picturesque pentagonal structure divided between the space for the orchestras and the space for the audience, which is covered by an illuminated ceiling of hundreds of luminous cylinders interspersed by canvases specifically destined to provide optimal acoustics. The **Kammermusiksaal** is to the left of the building, built by Wisniewski between 1984 and 1987 and reserved for chamber music. Its nickname is Kleine Philarmonie, little philharmonic. The building to the right, finished in 1984 on the design of Scharoun and Wisniewski and connected to the Philharmonie, holds the Musikinstrumenten - Museum. The museum, organized based on cutting-edge exhibition and educational concepts, lets visitors admire hundreds of instruments and go through the history of musical science from the 16th century to modern times through a rich library and specialized archive.

◀ **Philharmonie**   ▼ **Kammermusiksaal**

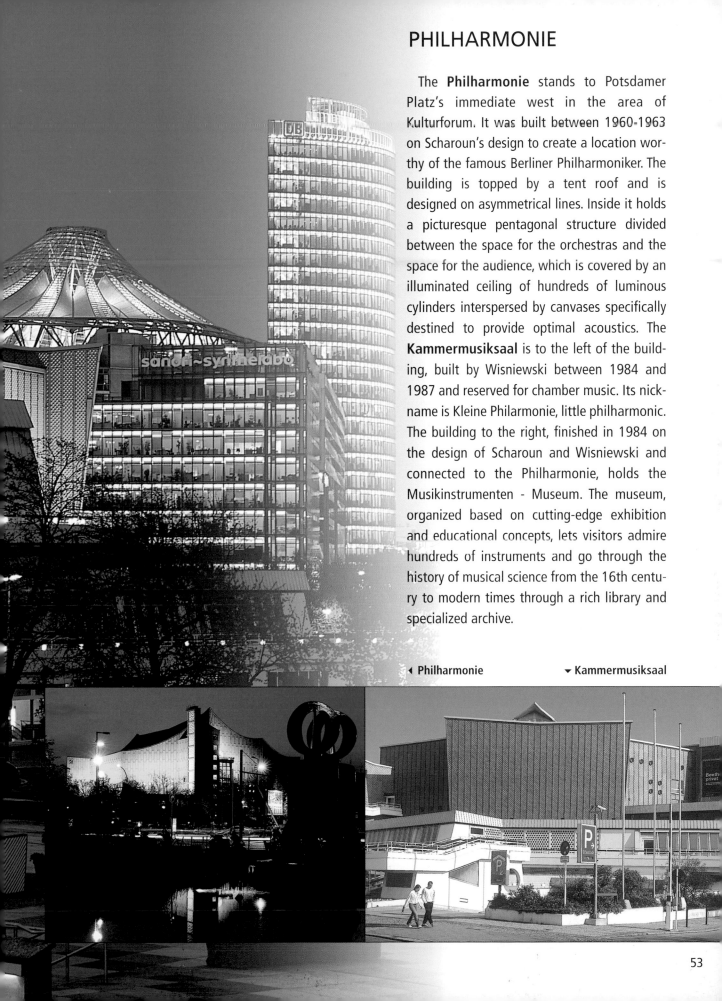

KURFÜRSTENDAMM

The wide avenue that runs between Rathenauplatz and Breitscheidplatz is the city's main commercial street. The Ku'damm, as Berliners call it, was originally a country road that Joachim II used to ride his horse between the castle and his hunting estate in Grunewald. In the 19th century, Bismarck had it paved and widened to a size to rival the Champs Elysées in Paris. The bombings of World War II ravished it, destroying almost all of the buildings that lined it. The few surviving buildings include the elegant early 20th century Iduna Haus and some sumptuous late 19th century buildings that stand in the middle of modern constructions built after the war. Lovers of shopping and strolling will find a memorable sight on the Ku'damm. Its sidewalks are always overflowing with street vendors and artists, lined by a succession of fashionable shops, elegant boutiques, fully-stocked department stores, cafes, nightspots, restaurants, hotels, cinemas, theatres and gathering places. Entertainment is a sure bet and only calms, like the intense traffic, late at night.

▲ Magic Balloon   Breitscheidplatz with the Globe Fountain ▶

BREITSCHEIDPLATZ

The square where the Ku'damm and three other large thoroughfares (Budapester Straße, Kantstraße and Tauentzienstraße) converge is easy to recognize for its **Globe Fountain** placed there in 1983. It is worth visiting especially for the remains of the Kaiser-Wilhelm **Gedächtniskirche**. The church was built in neo-romantic style by Franz Schwechten between 1891 and 1895 and was decimated by bombing on November 23, 1943. Only a part of the bell tower survived, which was originally 113 meters high and reduced to only 68 meters after losing its upper part. In the late 1950s, Egon Eiermann was asked to design a building that protected and highlighted the remains of the tower. Its original octagonal structure with blue panes covered with a flat roof and flanked by a hexagonal tower was built in only three years and consecrated in 1961. Since the late 1980s, the truncated

tower has held the Gedenkhalle, a memorial hall in which there is an effecting Christ made by Fritz Schaper in 1895 that stands alongside period photographic displays and fragments of the mosaic and sculptural decoration of the original church.

The square holds another original project from the 1960s, the **Europa Center**, a large shopping center designed by K.H. Pepper, built between 1963 and 1965. The center's total area of just under 100,000 square meters holds 22 floors of shops, boutiques, movie theatres, the prestigious Hotel Palace, a theatre and the famous "Die Stachelschweine" cabaret, as well as various offices and the headquarters of Berliner-Touristinformation. The view is marked by an interesting water clock made by Bernard Gitton.

Not far away, along the Ku'damm, the Kranzler-Eck, which takes its name from the famous **Café Kranzler**, provides a view of the city's chaotic traffic and the Gedächtniskirche on Breitscheidplatz.

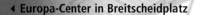

▲ Europa-Center - Water clock
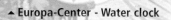

▲ Kranzler-Eck

From Breitscheidplatz, walking a short ways on Kantstraße, you reach the 19th century **Theater des Westens**, where the legendary Joséphine Baker performed in 1926.

SKULPTURENBOULEVARD

This outdoor sculpture gallery was created in 1987 for the 750th anniversary of the foundation of Berlin. It stretches along Ku'damm and the Tauentzienstraße as well as the two squares located at the opposite ends of the Ku'damm – Breitscheidplatz and Rathenauplatz – where the works of many contemporary artists have been displayed. Some of the most noteworthy works include Two Lines Excentric Joined With Six Angles by George Rickey, Grosse Frauenfigur Berlin by Rolf Szymanski and Pyramide by Josef Erben.

▼ Kranzler-Eck

Theater des Westens ▶

HANC DOMVM ARTIS COLENDAE CAVSA CONDIDIT.
ANNO MDCCCLXXXXVI BERNHARD SEHRING.

ZOOLOGISCHER GARTEN AND BAHNHOF ZOO

Not far from Breitscheidplatz, the **Berlin zoo** developed starting in 1844 after Frederick Wilhelm IV donated animals from his pheasant farm in Tiergarten and the animals that populated the Pfaueninsel. In the following centuries, it was greatly expanded and equipped with new facilities, including an aquarium, to become one of the largest and most important zoos in Europe. It was almost completely decimated during World War II. The reconstruction started after the war based on modern organization and breeding standards, favoring outdoor environments that reflected the natural habitats of the different animals as faithfully as possible. Starting in the late 1950s, the new spaces and buildings were further expanded and improved. Today it holds just under 14,000 animals and over 1500 species, making it the zoo populated by the largest number of species in the world. The rich Aquarium has been modernized and expanded with the addition of a terrarium and insectarium, holding about 12,000 animals from 500 different species.

West Berlin's most important station is near the **Bahnhof Zoologischer Garten**. The station was restored and modernized in the late 1980s. It was described along with the surrounding area in the autobiography We Children from Zoo Station, in which the protagonist Christiane F. illustrated her experience with drug addiction, violence and prostitution with the "Bahnhof Zoo" in the background.

▾ **Zoologischer Garten** ▸

▲ Bahnhof Zoologischer Garten

63

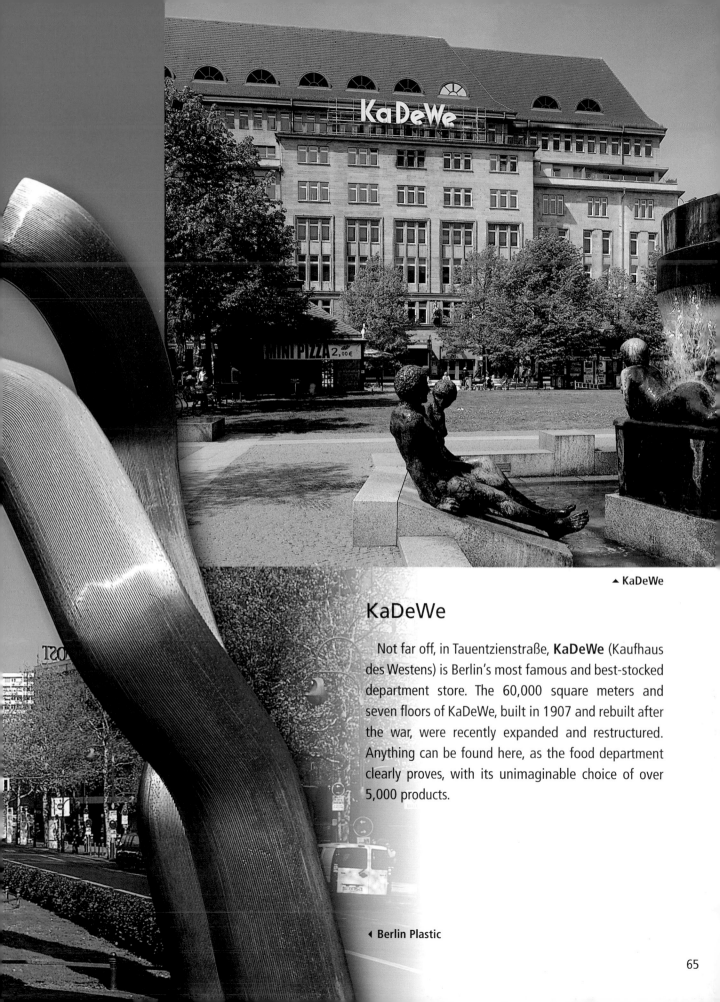

▲ KaDeWe

KaDeWe

Not far off, in Tauentzienstraße, **KaDeWe** (Kaufhaus des Westens) is Berlin's most famous and best-stocked department store. The 60,000 square meters and seven floors of KaDeWe, built in 1907 and rebuilt after the war, were recently expanded and restructured. Anything can be found here, as the food department clearly proves, with its unimaginable choice of over 5,000 products.

◀ Berlin Plastic

SCHLOSS CHARLOTTENBURG

Commissioned to Nering at the end of the 17th century by Frederick III, what was intended as a "simple" summer home for his second wife, Sophie Charlotte, turned over a century – which is how long it took to complete it – into one of Berlin's most sumptuous palaces. The castle is truly a summation of Prussian architecture in which the genius of the architects who helped build it can be recognized: Nering, the architect of the original building; Grünberg, who designed the two side wings; Johann Eosander von Goethe, to whom we owe not only the central overhang of the façade and the dome, but the Orangerie; Knobelsdorff, who added the wing along the eastern side with the party halls; Langhans, who designed the theatre near the winter garden; and finally Boumann, who worked on it at the end of the 18th century.

The view of the **Schloss Charlottenburg**, severely damaged by bombings in 1943 and then completely restored, starts from the Ehrenhof, in whose center stands the equestrian statue by Schlüter of the Grand Elector Wilhelm of Brandenburg.

The Historische Räume, the sumptuously furnished and decorated royal apartments, are in its central core. To the left of the wide vestibule and the luxurious oval hall are the apartments of Frederick III and his wife, including the spectacular Porzellankabinett. To the right, there is a hall of mirrors and various rooms decorated with gorgeous tapestries and the oak gallery. From here, a vestibule accesses the wing added by Knobelsdorff, with ballrooms in Rococo style, an elegant dining room and the amazing Goldene Galerie. Frederick II's apartments on the upper floor are furnished with precious works of art inspired by Etruscan art, Chinese porcelains and 18th century French paintings.

At the end of the western wing, the former court theatre is now

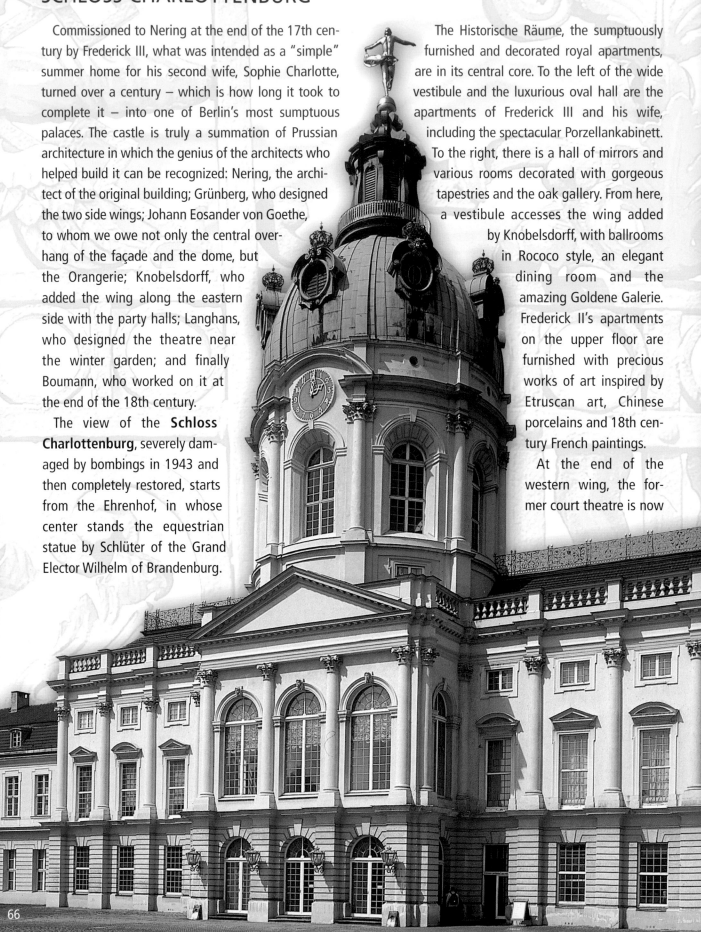

cent park that extends around the castle, was designed in French style by Siméon Godeau in the late 17th century and modified in English style by Johann August Eyserbeck and in 1819 by Peter Josef Lenné. The park area closest to Schloss Charlottenburg was redone in its original Baroque French style during the repair work after the war. The vast garden is interspersed by pools and stretches towards the banks of the Spree. Here you can admire the **Schinkel Pavillon**, built in 1825 as the summer home for Frederick Wilhelm III; the Belvedere, designed in the late 18th century Langhans as a teahouse, is the current site of a beautiful porcelain exhibition; and the mausoleum of Queen Louise, built in 1812 and expanded in the late 19th century.

the site of a museum with an interesting collection of prehistoric and antiquity art; on the upper floor, the Schliemann Saal displays many findings from excavations in Troy donated to the city by the archeologist Heinrich Schliemann in 1881. At the opposite end, on the ground floor of the wing added by Knobelsdorff in the mid 18th century, the Galerie der Romantik is dedicated to German painting of Romanticism, Classicism and the Biedermeier. The Schlosspark, a magnifi-

▾ Schloss Charlottenburg -
Shinkel Pavilion

▾ Victory Column (Siegessäule)

TIERGARTEN

The Otto-Suhr-Allee leads from the Schloss Charlottenburg to the Ernst-Reuter-Platz where the long, wide Straße des 17. Juni avenue begins.

The Hansaviertel skirts it in the direction of the gate Brandenburg. This residential neighborhood was leveled during the war and its reconstruction, started in the 1950s, was worked on by a group of world-famous architects including Gropius, Alvar Aalto and Niemeyer. The Kaiser-Friedrich-Gedächtniskirche stands out among its projects for its daring originality and its transparent belltower. It was built in 1957 by Ludwig Lemmer on the site of a previous 19th century church that was destroyed during the war.

Further up, Großer Stern is adorned in the center by the **Siegessäule** (1873), moved here from the Platz der Republik (formerly Königsplatz) in 1939. The majestic column is 69 meters high and crowned by a golden statue of victory. The theme of victory also appears on the bronze reliefs that adorn the base, marked by columns through which a mosaic can be seen portraying the foundation of the German empire. Inside, a stairway leads to a scenic terrace with a beautiful view of the Tiergarten.

The **Tiergarten** park spreads over 200 hectares. In the 17th century it was already a royal

▾ Tiergarten and view over Berlin

lung for the city. Between the 19th and 20th centuries, many monuments were built here, including one to Frederick Wilhelm III, statues of Goethe, Queen Louise, Bismarck and Wagner and a monument to Mozart, Haydn and Beethoven. Commemorative stones to Rosa Luxemburg and Karl Liebknecht can also be found in the park.

The **Kongresshalle** is also in the area of the Tiergarten, near the Spree and was designed by Hugh A. Stubbins with Werner Düttmann and Franz Mocken, built in 1957. Emphasized by a beautiful overhang roof, its futuristic lines make it one of the 20th century's architectural masterpieces. It is reflected in the pool in front of it, mixing with the reflection of Henry Moore's Two Figures sculpture, which has an equally soft, supple contour.

hunting estate, laid out in English-style by Lenné in the 19th century and opened to the public by Frederick II. The vast stretch, cleaved by waterways includes clearings, pools, fields and over 20 kilometers of paths. Though it was not spared by the bombs of World War II, it suffered the worst damage in the winter of 1946-47 when the people of Berlin fell most of its tree to get wood to burn. Through reforestation and repair work started after the war, the park has now been returned to its lush appearance and its role as a large green

▼ Haus der Kulturen der Welt (formerly Kongresshalle)

FRIEDRICHSTRAßE

Friedrichstraße, one of Berlin's other major thoroughfares, winds for over 3 kilometers between Oranienburger Tor, to the north, and Mehringplatz, to the south. The road was originally used for military parades and developed most between the late 18th century and early 19th century, when it gained buildings and shops as well as cafes, nightspots and theatres. Partly replaced by Kurfürstendamm in the 1920s, it was ravaged by Allied bombings on February 3, 1945, which razed almost all of its buildings, leaving it destroyed and abandoned. The construction of the Wall in 1961 dealt another hard blow to Friedrichstraße, which ended up cut in two at Zimmerstraße, about half way through it. Its reconstruction was started after the war and gained ground after the fall of the Wall and reunification with the help of many private investors. Unlike with Potsdamer Platz, here the authorities imposed specific architectural constraints.

▲ Friedrichstadtpalast   ▼ Bahnhof Friedrichstraße

The road starting at Oranienburger Tor quickly reaches **Friedrichstadtpalast**, a large theatre for variety shows built in 1984. The building was constructed on the site of a previous theatre, founded by Max Reinhardt in 1919 using the area of an older indoor market that dated back to 1868 and was turned into a circus in the imperial era.

Not far away, Weidendammbrücke, built in the late 19th century, brings together the two banks of the Spree with its 80 meters decorated by elegant wrought iron bulwarks.

A little further on, near the Unter den Linden, the **Bahnhof Friedrichstraße**, opened in 1822, served as the main border passage between the two sections of the city for the entire period in which Berlin was divided by the Wall.

▼ Friedrichstraße with Lafayette department stores

Along with the Unter den Linden, Friedrichstraße is a good illustration of the construction fever that has overtaken the city in recent decades, displaying urban and architectural projects of great originality. Points of particular interest in the area between the Französische Straße and Mohrenstraße include the Friedrichstadtpassagen, formed of complexes connected to one another ("Quartier") designed by different architects and defined by different purposes of use, mainly commercial and office. The central complex, **Quartier 206**, is the work of the Americans Pei Cobb Freed & Partners with a spectacular glass roof from which light filters, perfectly highlighting the intriguing color and geometric effects made inside with the use of marbles of various types and colors. The theme of lighting and plays of light reappears in the north complex, Quartier 207 by the French architect Jean Nouvel, which contains the **Galeries Lafayette**. In the center

Gendarmenmarkt – German Cathedral (Deutscher Dom) ▸

of the large department store, a funnel of enormous proportions stands 37 meters high made entirely of glass on whose surface the sparkling lights of the shops reflect to create truly spectacular effects.

Gendarmenmarkt opens up right behind Friedrichstadtpassagen, one of Berlin's most admired, elegant squares. The square has 17th century origins and owes its name to a regiment of gendarmes whose lodgings and stables it held for fifteen years in the 18th century. The major damage inflicted by bombings in World War II were repaired in the first years after the war, when

the Gendarmenmarkt was rechristened Platz der Akademie, which it abandoned in favor of its original name after the fall of the Wall. Of the three monumental buildings on the square, the oldest are the two cathedrals, built respectively in 1701-1705 and between 1701 and 1708, while the Schauspielhaus dates to the 1920s.

The **Französischer Dom** was designed by Louis Cayart and Abraham Quesnay, built on the north side of the Gendarmenmarkt for the community of exiled Huguenots who had moved to Prussia and Berlin in 1685. The majestic domed tower built in the late 18th century holds a small vinery

in about a third of its total height (70 meters) and a terrace with a spectacular view of the city twenty meters above. Inside the cathedral, you can visit an interesting museum dedicated to the history of the Huguenots.

In the same early 18th century years, on the square's southwestern side, the **Deutscher Dom** was built for the community of Lutheran Protestants in Berlin. As with the Huguenot cathedral, a dome tower was added the original structure designed by Martin Grünberg around 1750; the dome a twin to that of the Französische Dom designed by the same architect, Carl Friedrich von Gontard. In the same period, the cathedral which holds an exhibition dedicated to the city's last two years of history, was expanded with the addition of an elegant portico defined by columns.

The **Schauspielhaus** is Gendarmenmarkt's architectural jewel, standing in the center of the square

◀ **Schauspielhaus – Detail of a façade statue**

framed by the two cathedrals. The majestic building designed by Schinkel, was built in just three years, starting in 1818, on the site of the Nationaltheater, an older theatre destroyed in a fire just a year earlier. The Schauspielhaus – renamed Konzerthaus – has a front adorned with an elegant façade decorated with reliefs and topped by statues of the muses, after restoration work started in 1984. Today it is used exclusively for symphonies, which it

holds in its vast neo-classical main hall and chamber music for which a special smaller hall is reserved. A group of marble statues located in front of the building, surrounded by highly elegant hand-crafted wrought iron balustrade, portrays the great poet Friedrich Schiller with personifications of philosophy, history, dramatic and lyric poetry at his feet.

◄ Schauspielhaus - Detail of a façade statue

CHECKPOINT CHARLIE AND THE BERLIN WALL

Along the route to Mehringplatz, past Leipziger Straße, Friedrichstraße meets Zimmerstraße, where where the Wall passed and the famous **Checkpoint Charlie** stood as a point of passage between East Berlin and West Berlin. Right at the corner of the two streets, the **Haus am Checkpoint Charlie** passed through dark years of repression and tragic escape attempts when the division of the city was experienced by this place, which has been immortalized in countless spy films.

Starting in 1952, the year in which the border was officially closed, the authorities of the Democratic Republic

▲ Friedrichstraße: souvenirs from the former DDR   ▲ Haus am Checkpoint Charlie

were faced with the problem of a major flight of refugees who tried to reach the West across the Berlin border. To stem this flood and stop any escape attempts of any kind – while propaganda was giving different explanations, often on the far side of believable – in 1961, the decision was made to build a wall that physically separated the eastern sector of the city from the three western sectors. The construction of the immense barrier assigned to the men of the Volkspolizei and the Volksarmee was completed very quickly. In the following years, it was gradually supplied with armed surveillance towers, alarm systems, bunkers and everything else needed to keep the entire border under the tightest control. Within just a few days, Berlin found itself cut in two from the north to south by a cement wall over 40 kilometers long and over 4 meters tall and another 100 kilometers of barbed wire and metal fencing. On one side were the eastern neighborhoods of Pankow, Prenzlauer Berg, Mitte, Friedrichshain and Treptow, and on the west those of Reinickendorf, Wedding, Tiergarten, Kreuzberg and Neukölln. The Wall's construction inevitably led to a series of side effects, including the interruption of traffic on over fifty connection thoroughfares and the closure of many underground stations in East Berlin, the so-called ghost stations whose exits were walled up. The terrible materialization of the metaphorical Iron Curtain still did not succeed in suffocating the deep yearning for freedom of many Berliners who tried in all kinds of ways to escape

79

regardless. Many managed to pass the wall, but thousands were injured while trying to escape, arrested and imprisoned. Over seventy people fell victim in their desperate attempt to shots fired by Volkspolizei who constantly patrolled the wall. Meanwhile, on the other side of the wall many Berliners and others expressed their dissent from the government organs of the DDR and support of their fellow citizens by thousands of graffiti scrawled on its surfaces.

On November 9, 1989, the images of an enormous crowd who crossed the Wall flooding the streets of West Berlin traveled the world and touched public opinion everywhere. Little more than a month later, on December 22, the reopening of the Brandenburg Gate symbolized the end of the division between East and West Berlin and began the great process of reunifying the two Germanies.

The Wall, which stood for 28 years, was completely destroyed in just a few days, first by the blows of hammers and picks by the citizens themselves and then by Berlin authorities who completed its razing. Aside from the many fragments that ended up in museums in different countries and in the homes of those who wanted to take a piece as a souvenir, few remnants remain to bear witness to an indelible part of the history of Berlin and all of humanity. One of these few remnants is a 1300 meter long piece along the Spree that was painted on the eastern side from artists from throughout the world and turned into the now famed, much frequented **East Side Gallery**.

ALEXANDERPLATZ

Named after Czar Alexander I in 1805 when he visited Berlin, the enormous square (which Berlins call simply "Alex") arose in the area during the 18th century when a livestock and wool market was set up here. The history of **Alexanderplatz**, including the heavy bombings in 1945, is documented in a series of murals painted in the Hotel Park Inn's underground passageway. At the end of the 1960s, East Berlin authorities decided to reorganize the area, making it five times bigger than its original size and surrounding it by buildings inspired by pure Soviet realism. Primary among these buildings is the huge Hotel Park Inn with 39 floors, 123 meters high. The famed **Weltzeituhr**, Erich John's **World Time Clock** was placed in the square 1969, the year in which the artist Walter Womacka built the Brunnen der Völkerfreundschaft fountain. Berlin's administration gave the architect Hans Kollhoff the task of renovating Alexanderplatz while drastically reducing its dimensions as part

of the urban restructuring of the city's main sites.

Karl-Marx-Allee starts from the square's eastern side, renamed as such in 1961, canceling out its old name, Stalin-Allee. The long thoroughfare was opened in the early 1950s, stretching east to the heart of the Friedrichshain area. It was the first street built by the Soviet regime of East Germany.

On June 17, 1953, the workers building the public housing buildings that line the avenue, having been forced to keep up a grueling work pace, declared a strike that was immediately bloodily repressed by armed Soviet troops.

▼ Weltzeituhr, the "World Time Clock"

FERNSEHTURM

The building is the highest in Berlin since 1969 when the television tower was built and can be clearly seen from anywhere in the city with its 368 meters. The structure was designed by the architects Fritz Dieter and Günther Franke. It includes a spectacular terrace from which a breathtaking view of the city can be enjoyed and a steel sphere placed 200 meters high holding a scenic rotating café that gives visitors a 360° view of Berlin.

▲ Alexanderplatz: Marienkirche

ROTES RATHAUS

The former city hall of East Berlin, now the Berliner Rathaus, is not far from the television tower, from which it is separated by a park adorned by a beautiful fountain dedicated to Neptune, god of the sea. Since 1991 it has held the offices of the mayor and governing authorities of the reunified city. The stately building, whose name "red city hall" is owed to the bricks that clad the outside, was built between 1861 and 1869. The architect H. Friedrich Waesemann designed it in neo-Renaissance style, creating a three-level structure topped above the main entrance by a watch tower 74 meters tall. The building holds three interior courtyards. It is entirely surrounded on the outside by a sculptured terracotta frieze that displays the highlights of Berlin's history since its foundation to the 19th century.

The Marx-Engels-Forum is on the opposite corner between the Rathausstraße and Spandauer Straße. The Forum is a vast square clearing shaded by large trees in which a bronze sculpture portraying Marx and Engels stands. The monument became a tourist destination when, after the fall of the Wall, an anonymous hand added to its base the words "Wir sind unschuldig" (We are innocent).

◀ Alexanderplatz: Fernsehturm

NIKOLAIVIERTEL

The neighborhood covers a large area southwest of Rotes Rathaus, bordered by Rathausstraße, Spandauer Straße, Molkenmarkt, Mühlendamm and Spreeufer, on the banks of the Spree, at the site where the city of Berlin was founded. The neighborhood and its buildings, gathered around Nikolaikirche, have a historic appearance that is in reality false as it was rebuilt in the 1980s based on an ambitious project conceived by the architect Günter Stahn to return the area to its old charm. The alleys and little streets of this picturesque pedestrian island are closed to traffic. It is lined by low houses with traditional historic architecture, giving visitors a chance to dip into the past and enjoy a quite, evocative atmosphere.

Walking along the teahouses, charming restaurants and many artisan workshops, you will inevitably come to **Nikolaikirche**, the oldest church in the city, in the center of the neighborhood. The building's long history goes back to around 1230, when a Christian Basilicata stood at this point consecrated to St. Nicholas, later equipped with a small cemetery. In the latter part of the 15th century, another church with

late Gothic styles was built in the same area, with three naves covered by a saddleback roof. The building, after much remodeling and reconstruction, was severely damaged during World War II. The only vestiges of the original medieval church are the large blocks visible on the western wall and a few remnants of frescoes from the same era. Inside, main points of interest are the beautiful Kötteritzkapelle, made in the late Renaissance, and some funeral monuments.

In addition to Nikolaikirche and the original layout of the streets, Nikolaiviertel other interesting sights. Knoblachhaus, to the right of the church, was rebuilt at the end of the 1980s. It is a fine example of Rococo architecture built around 1760, along with the nearby Ephraim-Palais, whose elegant curved façade was also designed in Rococo style by Friedrich Wilhelm Diterichs. Veitel Heine Ephraim was built for Frederick the Great's treasury and is now an exhibition center. In the area you can admire the Drachentöter, an 1853 monument portraying St. George slaying the dragon.

▲ Nikolaiviertel

OBERBAUMBRÜCKE

From Nikolaiviertel, moving east along the Spree you reach **Oberbaumbrücke**, the bridge connecting the Kreuzberg neighborhood with Friedrichshain. When the city was divided by the Wall, it served as a walkway between East and West Berlin. On November 9, 1989, a crowd of citizens from the eastern section gathered under the shadow of its two enormous towers and celebrated the reopening of the border pouring onto the bridge to get to West Berlin.

In Treptow, a little to the south, on the banks of the Spree fans of modern sculpture can linger to admire the spectacular Molecule Man by the American artist Jonathan Borofsky, a colossal 30 meter high statue that is the largest outdoor sculpture in Berlin.

◀ **Molecule Man sculpture**

KULTURFORUM

Kulturforum is another project that fully expresses all of the incredible energy that runs through Berlin and its people. The English architect James Stirling defined it, colorfully, but accurately, as "the largest architectural zoo in the world". The complex was designed by the German architect Hans Scharoun in the 1950s and built in a vast area between the south side of the Tiegarten, Potsdamer Platz and Landwehrkanal, completely destroyed by bombings in World War II. The complex groups Berlin's museums dedicated to art and European culture. Its various structures came to be between the 1960s and 1990s, designed by architects of undoubted world fame the likes of Mies van der Rohe, Hans Scharoun and Edgar Wisniewski. Right after the Philharmonie, Hans Scharoun made the Staatsbibliothek between 1967-1978 in a vast area beyond Potsdamer Straße, which was turned from its original axis for the project. The rooms of the huge library preserve an impressive collection of works which belonged to the Preußische Staatsbibliothek. Over the years, a great many acquisitions have been added to bring the overall collection to an estimated four million items, including volumes, miniatures (including the 16th century Book of Hours by the Flemish Nicolas Firmian), ancient European and Asian manuscripts, autographed musical scores, maps and atlases.

The **Neue Nationalgalerie**, to the east of library, bears the signature of one of the greatest modern architects, Ludwig Mies van der Rohe. The building was built between 1965-1968. It is a highly linear glass and steel cube supported on a gray granite base. Its spaces hold works of painting, sculpture and contemporary graphics, providing a wide overview of varied European and American art in the 20th century. Outside behind the building is a fascinating open-air museum that features sculptures by Calder, Moore, Avramidis and Rickey where many temporary exhibitions are put on periodically by the gallery.

From the Neue Nationalgalerie, passing **St. Matthäus-Kirche**, which was designed by Stüler in the mid 19th century, you reach Kupferstichkabinett, opened in 1994. This rich museum includes an enormous number of drawings, watercolors, pastels,

▲ Neue Nationalgalerie

◄ St.-Matthäus-Kirche

engravings, manuscripts and illustrated volumes and an important collection of incunabula made from the medieval to the present day. The list of artists represented is quite impressive, including Botticelli, Dürer, Altdorfer, Bruegel the Elder, Rembrandt, Rubens, Tiziano, Piranesi, Callot, Watteau, David, Gainsborough, Goya, Van Gogh and Picasso. Kunstbibliothek, founded in 1867, is in the same complex and serves as a storehouse of information about applied and decorative arts with important collections of historic and modern architecture models, graphics and design.

The **Gemäldegalerie**, completed in 1998, is to the left of the Kupferstichkabinett and Kunstbibliothek. Its vast collection of pictorial works from the 13th to 18th centuries includes major paintings belonging to Frederick Wilhelm and Frederick the Great. A visit to the museum provides a spectacular trip through the major masterpieces of German, Flemish, Dutch, Italian, French and Spanish painting with priceless works including the likes of Dürer, Cranach the Elder, Holbein, Rembrandt (of whom Gemäldegalerie holds the beautiful Susanna and the Elders), Franz Hals, Vermeer, Hieronymus Bosch, Van Eyck, Hans Memling, Rubens, Giotto, Beato Angelico, Raffaello, Pollaiolo, Guardi, Canaletto, Mantegna, Tiziano, Veronese, Carpaccio, Tiepolo, Poussin, Pesne, Watteau, El Greco, Goya, Murillo and Zurbarán.

Finally, there is the Kunstgewerbemuseum was started in 1973 and completed in 1985 on the basis of the controversial design by Rolf Gutbrod, the architect who designed the exterior of the Gemäldegalerie. Its four floors hold a vast collection of applied and decorative art works from the Middle Ages to the present day. In addition to bronzes, glasses, ceramics and porcelain, visitors can admire works of gold and silversmithery, tapestries, furniture and historic and modern artisan objects.

▾ Hamburger Bahnhof

HAMBURGER BAHNHOF

Hamburger Bahnhof is located north of Kulturforum, past Straße des 17. Juni. It is Berlin's oldest station built between 1845-47 by Friedrich Neuhaus and Ferdinand W. Holz. The building is in neoclassical style and features an attractive atrium with an exposed iron framework. It was renovated by Josef P. Kleihues and now houses the Museum für Gegenwart, a section of the Neue Nationalgalerie that is counted among one of the most important contemporary art museums in Europe.

JÜDISCHES MUSEUM

The **Jewish Museum**, the work of Daniel Libeskind, takes its original, sharp lines from the star of David. The building is one of the most modern, daring and controversial of the projects in Neues Berlin. Its interior rooms, which are also designed on the theme of corners and edges, full and empty spaces as a metaphor of for the Holocaust, illustrate the history of Jews in Germany.

▲ Sammlung Berggruen

SAMMLUNG BERGGRUEN

Housed in western Stülerbau, across from the Ägyptisches Museum, the collection of modern painting by the great art dealer and collector Heinz Berggruen is one of the richest and finest in the world. In addition to a substantial core of paintings by Picasso, Berggruen's personal friend (including the famous The Seated Harlequin from 1905), the collection includes works by Klee, Van Gogh, Cézanne and other masters of modern painting.

MUSEUM FÜR KOMMUNIKATION BERLIN

This brand-new museum occupies the rooms in which the Reichspostmuseum was set at the end of the 19th century, along Leipziger Straße, in Mitte. Its displays cover the building's four floors and include a fine internal courtyard. Its interesting collection of objects and original tools illustrate the history of communications, starting with postal service to modern media and telecommunications, without overlooking their effects on society and everyday life.

▶ Museum für Kommunikation

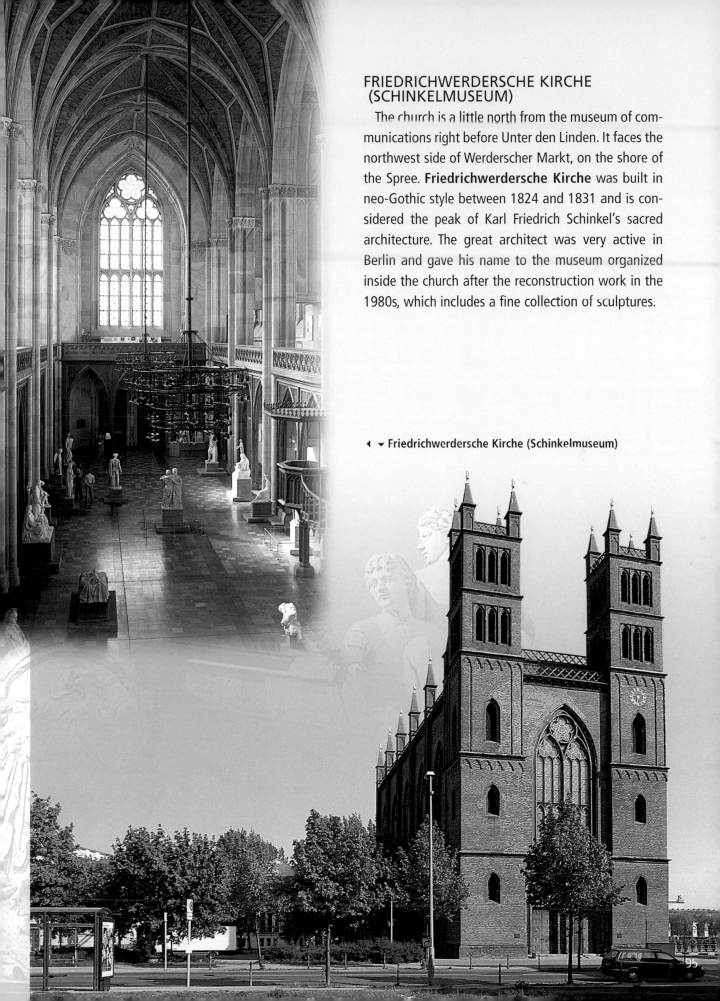

FRIEDRICHWERDERSCHE KIRCHE (SCHINKELMUSEUM)

The church is a little north from the museum of communications right before Unter den Linden. It faces the northwest side of Werderscher Markt, on the shore of the Spree. **Friedrichwerdersche Kirche** was built in neo-Gothic style between 1824 and 1831 and is considered the peak of Karl Friedrich Schinkel's sacred architecture. The great architect was very active in Berlin and gave his name to the museum organized inside the church after the reconstruction work in the 1980s, which includes a fine collection of sculptures.

◄ ▼ Friedrichwerdersche Kirche (Schinkelmuseum)

MESSEGELÄNDE

Berlin's large fair center hosts exhibitions of major import such as the International Turismusbörse (International Tourism Fair in March), the International Funkausstellung (radio and television trade fair and expo in August) and Grüne Woche (agricultural week in January). It covers an area of 150,000 square meters. Thirty pavilions are organized around the vast central Sommergarten, an oval summer garden. The **Messe** also includes several parking lots and the Deutschlandhalle to the south, a large multi-purpose complex used mainly for sporting events and concerts, and the nearby Eissporthalle skating rink. **The ICC, the International Congress Centrum**, dating from the 1970s, is east of the Messe, to which it is connected on three levels that cross the Messedamm and a line of the S-Bahn. The mammoth structure is over 300 meters long. It contains some eighty conference rooms, an enormous main hall that can hold up to 5,000 people, a restaurant, a bar, a post office, a police station and a variety of other services.

▲ **ICC, Internationales Congress Centrum**

The **Funkturm** is also inside the Messegelände and opened on September 4, 1926 for the third German radio tele-phony show. The tower is over 140 meters high and famed as the place where the first television image in history was broadcast. A scenic restaurant set 55 meters up and the terrace at 125 meters provide a breathtaking view of the fair neighborhood and the city.

▾ **South entrance to fairgrounds**

Funkturm ▸

NEUE SYNAGOGE (CENTRUM JUDAICUM)

The synagogue was built between 1860 and 1866 along Oranienburger Straße, in the Mitte neighborhood, designed by Eduard Knoblauch and Friedrich August Stüler. The building was made in Mooresque-Byzantine style and topped by a spectacular gold and silver dome. It could hold up to 3,000 faithful and was the largest synagogue in the world. During the brutal raids by Hitler's SA on the tragic Kristallnacht (between November 9 and 10, 1938), it only sustained a little damage, but it was destroyed by Allied air raids in 1943. After years of being abandoned, reconstruction work on the façade was started in 1988 and completed in 1991 for the 125th anniversary of the synagogue's foundation. Since 1995, when the interior restorations were finished too, the **Neue Synagoge** has held the **Centrum Judaicum**, as well as serving as a place of worship, the official headquarters of the Berlin Jewish community, and a museum and memorial to Berlin Jews and an active historic/scientific research center.

The surrounding neighborhood is bustling and full of buildings and interesting places to visit including the Kulturzentrum Tacheles, a large early 20th century building turned into an alternative art and culture center; the Jüdischer Friedhof, the first Jewish cemetery in Berlin (1672) of which, after the atrocities perpetrated by the Nazis in 1943, only a few headstones remain, including that of the philosopher Moses Mendelssohn; the Sophienkirche, which Queen Sophie had built in 1712 and is adorned by the city's oldest Baroque tower; **Hackesche Höfe**, a residential complex in Jugendstil built in 1907 on the design of August Endell which is

organized around eight completely renovated courtyards that now hold famous art galleries, workshops
and ateliers of artists and artisans, fine, fashionable
shops, cafes, restaurants and cinemas and theatres,
including one where you go to enjoy the famous
variety show "Camäleon".

▲ Mauergedenkstätte

Gedenkstätte Berliner Mauer is reached by following Oranienburger Straße north beyond the Oranienburger Tor, at the intersection of Invalidenstrasse and Bernauer Straße. It is one of the few surviving pieces of the Wall, which serves as a memorial another with other sections preserved near Mauerpark, on the corner of Bernauer Straße and Eberwalder Straße, and at the Invalidenstraße.

KREUZBERG

This neighborhood, which developed in the 1920s, took its name from the hill on which the beautiful Viktoriapark stretches. It has lost much of its interest that even just ten years ago made it Berlin's alternative neighborhood par excellence, the domain of the counter-culture, social centers and the most eccentric nightspots. The fall of the Wall determined a new placement for Kreuzberg, no longer at the edges of the city, but in the very center of Neues Berlin, with all of its contradictions and deep changes. This is not to say that the neighborhood, which has become markedly multi-ethnic, is not still one of the most interesting and authentic places in Berlin, partly for its very ability to show the many faces of this constantly changing city. Kreuzberg is crossed by the U-Bahn on an elevated line and by the Landwehrkanal and is connected to the Friedrichshain neighborhood by the Oberbaumbrücke. It is a great neighborhood to walk through, discovering along the Bergmannstraße, Mariannenplatz or the Maybachufer the bustling Turkish market, picturesque corners that are still infused with an elegant 19th century atmosphere alongside workshops and artistic centers of the alternative and underground culture, walls covered by graffiti and architectural pieces from the 19th century, traditional pubs along with the hippest of bars.

▼ Kreuzberg

OLYMPIASTADION

The complex was built by the architect Werner March for the Olympics in 1936. It was here that Jesse Owens achieved his legendary accomplishments. It was built between 1934 and 1936 on the site of a previous stadium built only twenty years earlier. The structure is original for the lowered main playing field, placed 12 meters below the level of the entrance (Olympiator). It includes over 76,000 covered seats. Through remodeling work concluded in 2004, the stadium was modernized for the 2006 World soccer championships.

SCHLOSS BELLEVUE

From Oranienburger Tor, going southwest down towards Straße des 17. Juni, at Großer Stern, dominated by Siegessäule, you find the Schloss Bellevue, which has held the official residence of the President of the German Republic since 1994. The castle is at the edges of the Tiergarten and was built in 1785 by Philipp Daniel Boumann for Prince August Ferdinand of Prussia. It was partially destroyed during World War II. After the Schloss Bellevue was rebuilt in the 1950s, it was expanded with the addition of an elliptical building with a façade entirely clad in black granite, where the President's offices are located. The castle and the English-style garden around it (with the exception of a small part) cannot be visited.

BOTANISCHER GARTEN

The botanical garden is the heart of the suburb of Dahlem, known primarily as the seat of Freie Universität, important scientific museums and famous museums (Museum für Indische Kunst, Museum für Ostasiatische Kunst, Museum für Völkerkunde). The garden developed between the 19th and 20th centuries, the work of Adolf Engler who made it one of the richest and famous gardens in the world. The garden extends over an area of over 40 hectares and has over 22,000 different plant species from throughout the world, including an incredible collection of tropical species in the Großes Tropenhaus, an enormous greenhouse in which the climatic conditions of the rain forest are reproduced. The Botanisches Museum is near one of the two entrances, equipped with a rich herbarium and an excellent specialized library. Its highly detailed dioramas illustrate the evolution of botanical species on earth.

MÜHLENDAMMSCHLEUSE

Mühlendammschleuse is near Ephraim Palais, past the Nikolaiviertel. It is the most important lock built in Berlin over the centuries to regulate traffic along the waterways within the city. Intense trade of all kinds of products through the river made it necessary to build many locks and mills. Mühlendammschleuse was destroyed in 1944 during the war and rebuilt in the 1960s. Today it is point of passage for large and small vessels.

PFAUENINSEL

Just 1500 meters long and about 500 meters wide, Peacock Island extends southwest from the Botanischer Garten in the Zehlendorf district, along the Havel river. The island is associated with the name of Johann Kunckel, an alchemist who conducted many experiments on this very spot in the late 17th century. In a vain attempt to create gold, he discovered phosphorous and made ruby glass (Kunckel glass). But Pfaueninsel owes its fame and much of its current beauty to Frederick Wilhelm II, who a century later had Lustschloss built here, a romantic white castle with two towers connected by an iron bridge and containing sumptuously decorated beautiful halls. Other buildings were added to the original construction over the years, including the Kavaliershaus, designed by Schinkel and later modified with the addition of a Gothic façade from Danzica, the Schweizerhaus, also by Schinkel, and the Vogelhaus, a large aviary populated by hundreds of birds. The island was turned into a beautiful English-style garden by Lenné and other landscape architects. Here Frederick Wilhelm II and his wife Louise created a small farm in which in addition to peacocks they had wild bears, monkeys and even some kangaroos. The little zoo was donated to city by Frederick Wilhelm IV in 1841 and formed the basis for the Zoologischer Garten.

◀ Pfaueninsel (Peacock Island), Lustschloss

WANNSEE

Wannsee is also in the Zehlendorf neighborhood. It is a wonderful suburb that emerged between the 19th and 20th centuries along the shores of the lake of the same name (Großer Wannsee), and is a favorite destination for Berliners to enjoy a few hours of relaxation on the beach or in the water, where they can practice water sports like sailing or just take a relaxing ride in a steamboat. Around the lake, pleasant paths are interspersed with elegant villas and homes nestled in the vegetation. In one of these homes, 56 Am Großen Wannsee, on January 20, 1942 the Nazis decided on the "final solution" of the Jewish problem. The house is now the site of a museum dedicated to the Holocaust. A regular ferry service runs from Wannsee to Spandau and Potsdam.

SPANDAU

Spandau is west of the center and developed at the convergence between the Spree and Havel rivers in an area that was annexed to Berlin only in 1920. The ancient town is formed of two cores: the Altstadt, the actual city on the western bank of the river where the 13th century Nikolaikirche and Gotisches Haus, the city's oldest house are found; and Zitadelle, the fortified city that was built in the latter part of the 16th century on the Zitadelleninsel.

The **Zitadelle** has a square layout and is protected along the sides by turreted bastions. It was designed by Italian and German architects and holds in various buildings the Kommandantenhaus, residence of the commandant, and the 13th century Palais across from it. Behind this building, which was turned into a casino for high officials during the Nazi period, is Juliusturm, a 14th century tower that is 36 meters high and provides a magnificent view, as does the walkway along the moat that borders the old Spandau lock.

◀ Spandau Citadel

BERLIN'S AIRPORTS

Berlin has three airports (Flughafen): **Berlin-Tempelhof**, in the city center right after Kreuzberg, **Berlin-Tegel** "Otto Lilienthal" in the northwest area and **Berlin-Schönefeld** on its southeast border. While the first is mainly for domestic flights, Tegel takes flights to and from Western Europe and the United States while Schönefeld serves as an airport for flights to Eastern Europe, the Middle East and Asia. Schönefeld is the focus a major expansion and improvement project to make it Berlin's main airport.

▲ Tempelhof airport
▼ Schönefeld airport

▲ Tegel airport

▲ Schönefeld airport

▲ Schönefeld airport

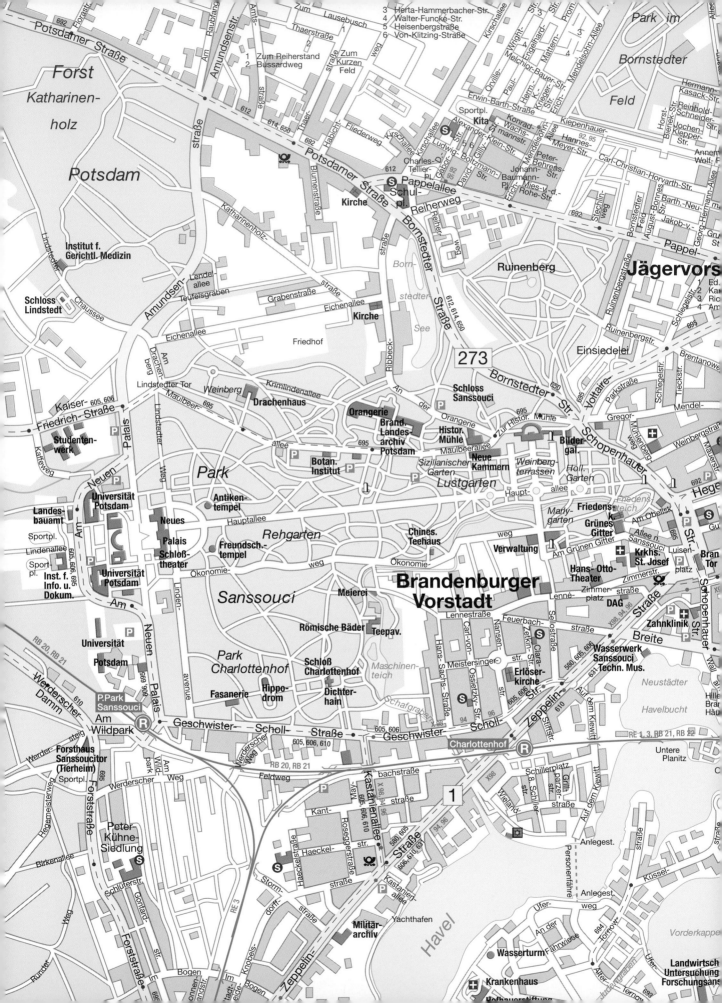

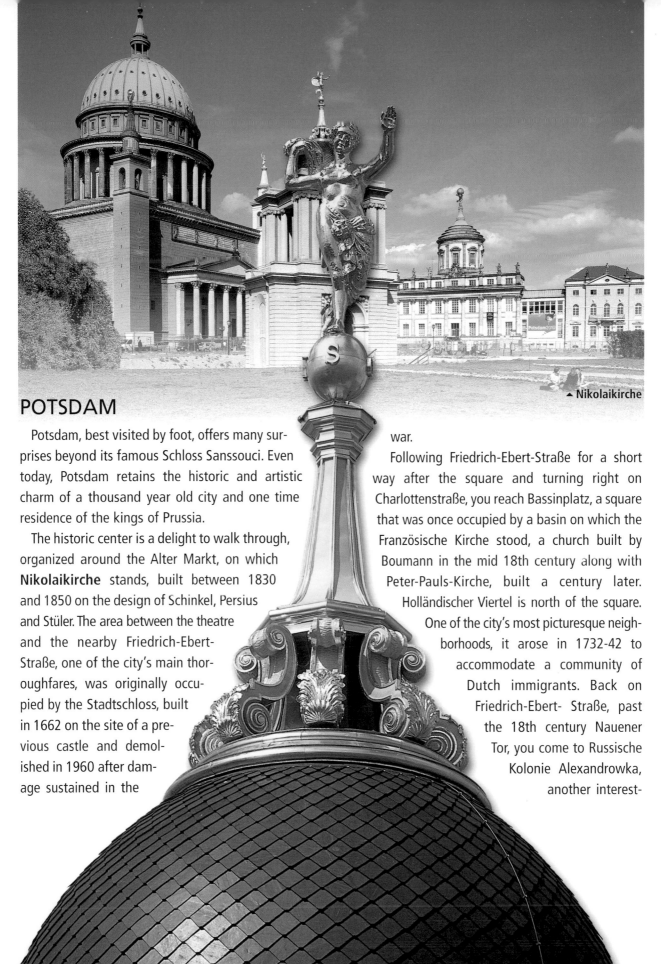

▲ Nikolaikirche

POTSDAM

Potsdam, best visited by foot, offers many surprises beyond its famous Schloss Sanssouci. Even today, Potsdam retains the historic and artistic charm of a thousand year old city and one time residence of the kings of Prussia.

The historic center is a delight to walk through, organized around the Alter Markt, on which **Nikolaikirche** stands, built between 1830 and 1850 on the design of Schinkel, Persius and Stüler. The area between the theatre and the nearby Friedrich-Ebert-Straße, one of the city's main thoroughfares, was originally occupied by the Stadtschloss, built in 1662 on the site of a previous castle and demolished in 1960 after damage sustained in the war.

Following Friedrich-Ebert-Straße for a short way after the square and turning right on Charlottenstraße, you reach Bassinplatz, a square that was once occupied by a basin on which the Französische Kirche stood, a church built by Boumann in the mid 18th century along with Peter-Pauls-Kirche, built a century later. Holländischer Viertel is north of the square. One of the city's most picturesque neighborhoods, it arose in 1732-42 to accommodate a community of Dutch immigrants. Back on Friedrich-Ebert- Straße, past the 18th century Nauener Tor, you come to Russische Kolonie Alexandrowka, another interest-

ing neighborhood founded in 1826 and defined by the traditional Russian architecture of its houses.

You can take Jägerallee to go downwards to the south. Past the Jäger Tor you find the Lindenstraße, a beautiful 18th century street that intersects with **Brandenburger Straße**, Potsdam's pedestrian area. The **Brandenburger Tor** (1770), at its westernmost point, in actuality shares little more than its name with the like-named more famous Berlin gate. This Tor is inspired to a more modest Roman arch of triumph. The Friedenskirche is nearby, past the nearby Luisenplatz. The church is the masterpiece of Ludwig Persius built between 1845 and 1848 on the model of proto-

▲ Brandenburger Tor   Altes Rathaus ▼

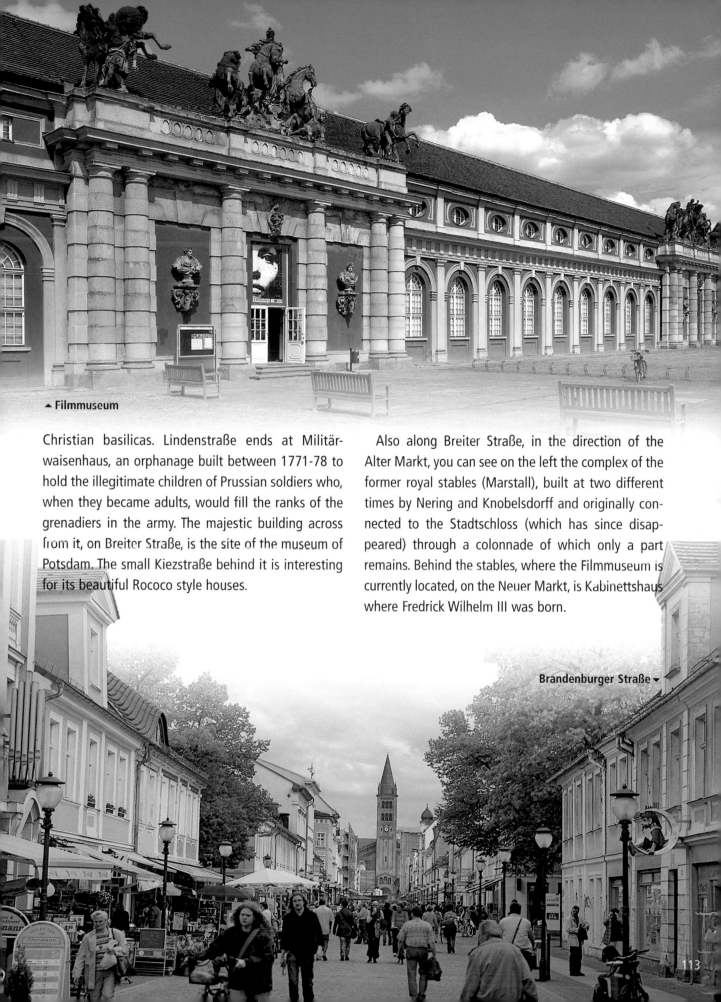

▲ Filmmuseum

Christian basilicas. Lindenstraße ends at Militär-waisenhaus, an orphanage built between 1771-78 to hold the illegitimate children of Prussian soldiers who, when they became adults, would fill the ranks of the grenadiers in the army. The majestic building across from it, on Breiter Straße, is the site of the museum of Potsdam. The small Kiezstraße behind it is interesting for its beautiful Rococo style houses.

Also along Breiter Straße, in the direction of the Alter Markt, you can see on the left the complex of the former royal stables (Marstall), built at two different times by Nering and Knobelsdorff and originally connected to the Stadtschloss (which has since disappeared) through a colonnade of which only a part remains. Behind the stables, where the Filmmuseum is currently located, on the Neuer Markt, is Kabinettshaus where Fredrick Wilhelm III was born.

Brandenburger Straße ▼

SANSSOUCI

North of Luisenplatz, the gate of the obelisk, built in 1747 by Knobelsdorff, gives entry directly to the main street of the **Sanssouci** park, embellished by splendid fountains. The building was also built by Knobelsdorff on Frederick II's own design between 1745 and 1747. It stands atop Wüste Berg, whose slopes had been recently turned into a terraced vineyard. The building, where the king would have been able to enjoy a few carefree moments (thus, "sans souci"), has modest dimensions and has just twelve rooms, including one that was the studio and bedroom where the king died. In the beautiful, marble-covered atrium with its beau-

▼ Sanssouci castle with busts of Bacchantes

▲ Sanssouci - Colonnade

New Chambers and Historic Mill ▲

tiful view of the vineyards, Frederick II loved to plan banquets here to which he invited the era's illustrious personages, such as Voltaire who lived in Potsdam between 1750 and 1753. Its library, which holds over 2,000 volumes, looks over the tomb that the king had built at the end of the terrace even before the

building was finished. His remains were transferred here only in 1991. The Bildergalerie was built by Büring in 1755-64 to the right of the building, holding the king's painting collection. The Neue Kammern, built to its left on Knobelsdorff's design in between 1745 and 1747, was used as a guest house.

▲ Neue Palais ▶

The **Neue Palais** is decidedly larger and more sumptuous. It is set in a picturesque location at the end of the avenue. It was built twenty years later with the express intent of reaffirming the power of Prussia after the Seven Year's War. Frederick II, who continued to favor the more intimate Sanssouci, commissioned its construction to the architects Büring, Manger and Gontard. Between 1763 and 1769 they built the stately palace with 200 rooms and a crowd of statues placed on its roofs. Behind it were the **Communs**, enormous buildings used to house the servants' quarters. The castle's richest and most spectacular rooms include the vast Grottensaal, decorated with thousands of gems, colored stones, shells, fossils and minerals that make it look like a marvelous grotto; the Marmorsaal, entirely clad in precious marbles; and the palace's theatre which is still used for plays and shows. Little is left of the lavish furnishings that originally adorned the different rooms. In 1918, Wilhelm II brought them almost all with him to Holland when he went in exile.

The Schloss Charlottenhof, on the other hand, main-

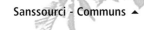

tains all of its original furnishings. Frederick Wilhelm IV had it built by Schinkel in 1826, when he was still crown prince, turning it from farm gifted by his father into a pleasure villa in Roman style. Soon after, Schinkel and Persius built the nearby Römische Bäder for the king, inspired by the Italian Renaissance country homes.

Orangerie ▼

The large **Orangerie** was another tribute to Renaissance style, introduced in Prussia by Frederick Wilhelm IV. It was built by Persius and Stüler between 1850-64. The beautiful building took inspiration from the Villa Medici in Rome and the Uffizi in Florence. It stands to the north along the Maulbeerallee, the avenue that winds between Belvedere and the old mill of Sanssouci. In the king's plans, it was intended as a kind of "via triumphalis". The Orangerie is worth visiting for the Raffaello hall, decorated by about sixty works by the great painter, as well as for its tower which offers a spectacular view of the park and its monuments.

Chinese tea pavilion

Meanwhile, the Drachenhaus, built by Gontard in 1770, and **Chinesische Teehaus** built in the mid 18th century further south on the edge of the park's main avenue, bear witness to the love for Oriental art and Chinese objects that exploded in the Rococo period.

▲ Chinesisches Teehaus
- gilt figures

◄ Chinesisches Teehaus

123

NEUER GARTEN

The Neuer Garten and Marmorpalais on the opposite side of the city are owed to Frederick Wilhelm II. Out of spite for his hated uncle Frederick the Great, for whom he bore a deep aversion, he abandoned the park of Sanssouci and had himself a pleasure home built in the area to the east of Potsdam on the shore of the Heiliger See. The king had Gontard build the palace of Marble, a neo-classical grandiose building that the architect constructed between 1787 and 1793. A romantic detail: from Marmorpalais Frederick Wilhelm II could admire the Pfaueninsel and especially the Lustschloss, the small white castle that he had built a few years later on the island of the peacocks for his lover Wilhelmine Encke, the future Countess of Lichtenau who bore him five children.

The park was originally laid out by Eysenbeck and later redesigned by the very active Lenné. It is perfect for enjoying a peaceful walk in green nature. Crossing the park, you come across a whole series of rather bizarre buildings. There is the Gotische Bibliothek, designed by Langhans at the eastern end of the lake, the Orangerie by the same architect and the Holländisches Etablissement, a large complex of stables and garages for his carriages. Highlights include the interesting Küchenhaus, a kitchen that looks more like an ancient small Roman temple connected to the Marmorpalais by an underground passageway and the Eiskeller, an ice house in the shape of an Egyptian pyramid.

The park and the strange architectures of the Neuer Garten had formed the backdrop of the king's joie de vivre – he was a man who decidedly loved the pleasures of life but who it seems also indulged happily in its worst vices (it was not for nothing that one of his contemporary had said that under his reign Potsdam had become a "giant bordello"). After the end of

▾ Schloss Cecilienhof ▸

World War II, they became the theatre of a much more serious and decisive event. In the summer of 1945, the top leaders of the victorious Allied forces (Truman, Stalin and Churchill) met at **Schloss Cecilienhof** for the famous Potsdam Conference to decide the fate of Germany and the future organization of Europe. The castle, completed in the years after World War I and intended for the son of Wilhelm II, the crown prince Wilhelm, now hold a luxury hotel with an attached restaurant. You can still visit the hall where the Conference took place. Everything, including the great table, brought from Moscow especially for the meeting, and was left as it was at the moment of the historic meeting.

BABELSBERG

Schloss Babelsberg is set a beautiful park, created by Lenné, almost needless to say, this time in collaboration with Fürst von Pückler-Muskau. It was built in neo-Gothic style by Schinkel in 1834 to hold the summer home of emperor Wilhelm I. Other interesting projects in neo-Gothic style other than the castle can be admired in the park including Küchengebäude (1844-49), the Matrosenhaus (1842), the Marstall (1842), the Flatowturm (1853-56) and the Kleines Schloss (1842), for the ladies of the court and now a fine cafe.

Babelsberg is famed for more than just these monuments and its wonderful garden. It is also the location of the famous DEFA-Filmstudios, which were created in 1917 as UFA. Today, Babelsberg's cinema city gives give visitors the chance to get a first hand look at the backstage, which includes everything that happens when a film is being made, from lighting, costumes, film takes, and the entire technical process.

INDEX

© **RAHMEL-VERLAG GmbH** – DE-50259 Pulheim
Telephone: +49 (0)2238 30 71-0 – Fax +49 (0)22 38 30 71-27
email: info@rahmel-verlag.de
http://www.rahmel-verlag.de

ISBN: 3-930885-66-2

Text: Claudia Converso
Translation: A.B.A. s.r.l.
Printing: Kina Italia / Eurografica Spa
All photos by Luca Sassi except for the following:
Ihlow: pages 16, 18, 40 (2), 83 (center), 101 (top), 102 (top),
105 (top) – Seitz: page 31 (bottom) – Latza: page 105 (bottom)
– Hoth: page 42 (top)